*This
Chronicle belongs*

*to:* _____

# CHRONICLES
## OF CHILDHOOD

# CHRONICLES
## — *of* —
# CHILDHOOD

◆

*Recording Your Child's
Spiritual Journey*

◆

**ELISA MORGAN**

**NAVPRESS**
A MINISTRY OF THE NAVIGATORS
P.O. BOX 35001, COLORADO SPRINGS, COLORADO 80935

The Navigators is an international Christian
organization. Jesus Christ gave His followers
the Great Commission to go and make disciples
(Matthew 28:19). The aim of The Navigators is to
help fulfill that commission by multiplying laborers
for Christ in every nation.

NavPress is the publishing ministry of The Navigators. NavPress publications are tools to help
Christians grow. Although publications alone cannot make disciples or change lives, they can help
believers learn biblical discipleship, and apply what
they learn to their lives and ministries.

Library of Congress Catalog Card Number:
     91-61427
ISBN 08910-96302

Second printing, 1992

Cover illustration: Gwen Connelley

Unless otherwise identified, all Scripture in this
publication is from the *Holy Bible: New International Version* (NIV). Copyright © 1973, 1978, 1984,
International Bible Society. Used by permission of
Zondervan Bible Publishers. Other versions used
include: the *Good News Bible: Today's English
Version* (TEV), copyright © American Bible Society
1966, 1971, 1976; and *The New Testament in Mod-
ern English* (PH), J. B. Phillips Translator, © J. B.
Phillips 1958, 1960, 1972, used by permission of
Macmillan Publishing Company.

Printed in the United States of America

FOR A FREE CATALOG OF
NAVPRESS BOOKS & BIBLE STUDIES,
CALL TOLL FREE 1-800-366-7788 (USA)
or 1-416-499-4615 (CANADA)

# CONTENTS

HOW TO RECORD YOUR CHILD'S JOURNEY

## PART ONE—FOOTPRINTS: A CHRONICLE OF THE HEART

### DEVELOPING CHARACTER
*Self-Control*
*Joy*
*Perseverance*
*Wisdom*

### LEARNING TO LOVE
*Love*
*Kindness*
*Forgiveness*
*Teachability*

### DISCOVERING GOD
*God Is Good*
*God Is Holy*
*God Is Gracious*
*God Is Faithful*

## PART TWO—STEPPINGSTONES: A CHRONICLE OF MEMORIES

*Questions About God*
*Prayers*
*Favorite Bible Stories and Verses*
*Meaningful Church Experiences*
*Significant Ministry Experiences*
*Mentors*
*Significant Losses*
*The Meaning of Christmas*
*The Meaning of Easter*
*Salvation*
*Baptism*
*Church Membership*

ROAD SIGNS FOR A SAFE JOURNEY

NOTES

*To Annie*

*Your journey was short
but oh, so sweet.*

# AUTHOR

Elisa Morgan is the executive director of Mothers of Preschoolers International (MOPS), which has over 500 chapters and ministers to over 16,000 women. She speaks about general Christian living on a daily five-minute radio program ("Considerations") that is broadcast by over 200 stations nationwide. She has an M.Div. in counseling and is the author of one book. Elisa and her husband have two preschool children.

# How to Record
# Your Child's Journey

◆

*Praise the LORD, O my soul,*
*and forget not all his benefits.*
PSALM 103:2

One December Sunday, after we'd returned home from church, my children asked Jesus to come and live in their hearts. We sat on the couch, discussed the miracle of God loving us enough to die on our behalf, and bowed our heads to welcome Jesus to the home of their hearts. My daughter was five at the time. My son was three.

While I was as touched as any mother would be at this momentous occurrence, doubts cast a shadow on the delight of my joy. *They're so young. Will this decision stick? When she's twelve, will she even remember this moment? When he hits sixteen, will he pull away in defiance, negating the reality of what happened here?* How could I help them recall this moment with the sincerity and unswerving commitment only a child could bring to it?

Our children are pilgrims in progress. Each day they awaken and embark upon the journey that is life. One step at a time, they move forward, then back, then forward again, as they explore and discover their identities, their world, and their God.

We parents wonder how we can set them off along the right path. We whisper directions under our breaths. We motion away from trouble and beckon toward health. We forecast failure ahead and lecture about past lessons learned. With necks craning to see around the next bend, we begrudgingly acknowledge that no matter how we prod and plead, we can't travel the journey for our children. Each must discover God on his own.

Yet, as "observer-scribes," we can *accompany* our children on their journey. Young lives may have difficulty recording their spiritual journey while they travel. The parent who walks alongside can record a son or daughter's steps toward God and one day offer back a reminder of what the child has learned along the way.

In his book *Ordering Your Private World*, Gordon MacDonald speaks of how writing his own account of his journey impacted his understanding of God.

> I am reminded that the Lord once had the Israelites save three quarts of manna (Ex. 16:33 TLB) so that they would have a tangible reminder of His constant care. The journal became my "three quarts" for in it I had all the testimony I needed to the faithfulness of God in my life.[1]

Like Joshua piling rocks taken from the Jordan River, remembering God's deliverance of the Israelites into the Promised Land with an altar, we can offer our children a chronicle of God's faithfulness throughout their childhood. We can keep a record of their journeys and give them a glimpse of God.

So now you're convinced. . . .

But how does this journal-keeping work? How can a mother who is already juggling the needs of a husband, two children, her own work, and pastimes take out more time to write a journal? How can a father, already coupling career and kids, move away the clutter and compose a chronicle?

Relax. This book has been created with you and your schedule in mind. There are several absolutes you must accept before you begin.

## NO GUILT

If you miss a month, that's okay. Don't worry about it. Write when you can. (You'll find that if you try to write too often, you'll run out of pages to accommodate all the years of your child's life!) If your child makes a marvelous remark on the way to the store, jot it down on the back of an envelope and stick it in the book. You can fill in the details later.

## No Grades

Points will not be deducted for misspelled words, incorrect sentence structure, or lack of punctuation. Don't get stuck back in eighth-grade grammar class.

## No Comparisons

There is not just one way to record a journal. You can whip out quick comments or compose prosaic verses. You can write once a month or once a year or skip five years and then come back strong. Whether your sister keeps her book completely up-to-date or doesn't crack it open after the baby shower doesn't have anything to do with you. Make the journal work your way and it will later work in the life of your child.

## No Pressure

Throughout this book you'll find comments, quotes, and questions to prod your thinking. If you're the type who likes to write from scratch, use these as launching pads for your own thoughts. On the other hand, if you prefer to be guided, let this book assist you in transferring your thoughts to the paper.

You'll notice that the book is divided into two main sections: Footprints—which contains sub-sections on character traits, relational skills, and understanding God's character—and Steppingstones, a place to record special events and memories. Throughout the Footprints section you'll find devotional-type essays on the topics and space to record pertinent observations or comments from your child's life. Each essay is followed by a prayer you may wish to voice for your child. Since there are twelve topics in the Footprints section, you may choose to work through one topic each month for a year and then begin again the next year, watching for the growth in your child from one year to the next.

You'll notice that the gender descriptions have been changed every other essay to make sure this book works for either a boy or girl. Please make allowance for this when you're praying for your child.

The Steppingstones section follows a fill-in-the-blank format and traces particular childhood events. An appendix is at the end, called

Road Signs for a Safe Journey. It contains developmental information you might find helpful in interpreting your child's progress in his journey toward God.

Need a few examples? In the Footprints section, under Developing Character, is *Perseverance.* You might write something like this:

*7/6/90*    *Susie rode her bike without training wheels for the first time tonight. Another milestone. As she got in the shower to wash off the sweat of achievement, she said, "I'm really proud of myself!" How healthy! How wonderfully free! She has seen the reflection of her abilities in our eyes! Thank You.*

Also in the Footprints section, under Discovering God, you'll see *God Is Faithful.* You might write:

*9/10/91*    *We searched all over the house for Brian's other shoe. It was nowhere to be found. Brian grabbed my arm and whispered, "Maybe we ought to pray to Jesus. I bet He knows where it is." He knew You to be faithful when I had forgotten.*

Then in the Steppingstones section, where the journey is charted by specific events, you could make entries like these:

*Questions About God*
*8/4/90*    *"Where is God?" Melanie asked after we'd had a chat a few days before about God watching over all she does.*

*Prayers*
*12/1/90*    *"Thank You that You love me even when I mess up." Scott prayed this after a particularly difficult day.*

*Significant Ministry Experiences*
*4/8/91*    *Matt volunteered our family to help with the Thanksgiving outreach for the inner-city people. He was*

*absolutely on fire to get us there and then worked with*
*abandon, stuffing brown sacks with vegetables and stuff-*
*ing. "We have so much," he said. "We've just got to do*
*something for those who don't."*

Have you got the idea? It's not complicated. It's not particularly time-consuming. In fact, it really requires very little on your part. All you have to do is record. Your child is the one who is providing something to write about.

Give it a try. You'll be glad you did when, at high school graduation or some other such launching event, you're able to place this record in the hands of your pilgrim. Keep a chronicle and give your child a glimpse of God.

# Part One

# FOOTPRINTS:
# A CHRONICLE
# OF THE HEART

*They are not monuments, but footprints.*
*A monument only says, "At least I got*
*this far," while a footprint says,*
*"This is where I was when I moved again."*
WILLIAM FAULKNER
*quoted in*
A Long Obedience in the Same Direction

# DEVELOPING
# CHARACTER

◆

*Sow a thought, reap an act;*
*Sow an act, reap a habit;*
*Sow a habit, reap a character.*
CHARLES READE

# SELF-CONTROL

◆

Peter the Great was the maker of Czarist Russia. He captured city upon city, but he never was able to hold his temper. Once, in a fit of rage, he murdered his own son. Near the end of his reign he commented, "I have conquered an empire, but I was not able to conquer myself."

Proverbs 16:32 says, "It is better to win control over yourself than over whole cities" (TEV). Surely Peter the Great wished he had claimed this verse as his own for life.

Most literally, the word *self-control* comes from two roots: one meaning to "rein in" or "curb" and the other meaning to "heal," "preserve," "make whole." These roots apply particularly to the sensitive nature of man: his mind. Putting it more simply, to be self-controlled is to be healthy-minded.

When Mark and Luke give account of the healing of the demoniac, healthy-minded or self-controlled is how they describe his condition after Jesus had cast the demons out of him. From an uncontrollable monster under the guidance of Satan, Legion became self-controlled, healthy-minded, through the healing of Jesus.

Satan would love to see us out of control, like Peter the Great or like the demoniac of the gospels. He would have us be ranting and raving replicas of our out-of-control society. So he attacks. Through the bent nature of the toddler, the autonomous strivings of the elementary school child, and the rebellious independence of the teenager, Satan rears his head to steer off-course the natural and necessary individuation of children from their parents. At times our child appears more like Czar Peter, more like the demoniac, than the babe we held in our arms.

Self-control begins with mind control. Gradually, over a period of trial and error, a child can learn to say no to the temptation of disorder. Little "monsters" can become disciplined individuals who delay gratification, order their schedules, and hold down part-time jobs.

Self-controlled children are those who are healthy-minded. With renewed and transformed minds they end up smarter than their Enemy.

---◆---

### PRAYER

*Dear Lord, please give my child self-control. Steel his mind with health so that he might make wise choices. Protect him with Your wisdom and truth so that he might think clearly about those dilemmas he faces. Help him learn to express emotions appropriately and without damaging others. Enable him to wait for what he wants, knowing that You are with him as much in the wait as You are in the fulfillment at its end. May I be a model of self-control that he might see in me an accurate reflection of this quality and how to put it into practice in everyday life. Amen.*

---◆---

◆

*Like a city whose walls are broken down*
*is a man who lacks self-control.*
PROVERBS 25:28

◆

---

DATE

---

DATE

---

DATE

---

DATE

◆

*Self-discipline is neither godliness nor is it the means to godliness.*
*If discipline led to godliness, the most disciplined individual would be*
*the holiest—and holiness would be a result of human works.*
D.G. KEHL
Christianity Today

◆

_____
DATE



_____
DATE




_____
DATE




_____
DATE

◆

*The end of all things is near. Therefore be clear minded
and self-controlled so that you can pray.*
1 PETER 4:7

◆

---
DATE

---
DATE

---
DATE

---
DATE

♦

*Be self-controlled and alert. Your enemy the devil prowls around
like a roaring lion looking for someone to devour.*
1 PETER 5:8

♦

DATE _____

DATE _____

DATE _____

DATE _____

♦

*Self-control is primarily mind control.*
JOHN STOTT
Your Mind Matters

♦

# JOY

"I've got the joy, joy, joy, joy down in my heart!"[1] What does it feel like to have joy down in your heart? What does it mean?

Joy is more than happiness. The word *happiness* comes from the root, "hap," which means "chance." Where happiness is circumstantial, joy is not.

Andrew Acquistapace, in *The Standard*, observes that the Old Testament describes joy as a quality of life as well as an emotion. The spontaneous songs of worship contained in the Psalms illustrate such joy. And in the New Testament, joy is often expressed as ecstasy, a feeling of amazement, an uninhibited response to the grace of God. The tidings of joy brought to the shepherds by the angels would be an example of this kind of joy.[2]

In chapter five of his letter to the Galatians, Paul speaks of joy in another sense as he challenges us to cooperate with God in the production of the fruit of the Spirit in our lives. The characteristics of the fruit of the Spirit—love, joy, peace, patience, etc.—are God-like qualities expressed in human personality. We attract others to the seed of the gospel when we allow God to grow the attractive fruit of His character in our lives.

Joy is one aspect of this fruit. The fruit of joy is an unshakable confidence in the truths of God, despite circumstances. When others see an unshakable confidence in the life of one who says he knows God personally, they are impressed and drawn to know Him themselves.

The philosopher, Friedrich Nietzsche, once criticized Christians by saying, "I would believe in their salvation if they looked a little more like people who have been saved." The fruit of the Spirit is produced to draw others to eat of the seed of the gospel. Joy is not a sentimental happiness dependent on chance, but a confidence rooted in the truth of God. If we want folks like Nietzsche to believe in our God, we'll need more than a pasted-on smile of chance happiness. Joy is a confidence in God despite circumstance.

---◆---

### PRAYER

*Dear Lord, please give my child a reason to taste the true joy of being confident in You. Show her the difference between the chance happiness of our world and the unshakable confidence of knowing Your character to be unchanging and true. And may this fruit of confidence be evidenced in my child's outlook, her attitudes, her bearing, and her being, that she might attract others to Your truth. Amen.*

---◆---

♦

*So with you: Now is your time of grief, but I will see you again*
*and you will rejoice, and no one will take away your joy.*
JOHN 16:22

♦

---

DATE


---

DATE


---

DATE


---

DATE

◆

*Joy is bedrock stuff. . . . Joy is a confidence that operates irrespective of our moods. Joy is the certainty that all is well, however we feel.*
CALVIN MILLER
Discipleship Journal

◆

DATE

DATE

DATE

DATE

♦

*If we have learned that He is perfectly wise, then we can trust Him for
our plans for our lives. If we know Him to be perfectly loving, then we can
believe Him even when something doesn't appear to be the product of His
love. To know Him as the Lord of our lives enables us to experience true joy.*
MARVA J. DAWN
Discipleship Journal

♦

---
DATE

---
DATE

---
DATE

---
DATE

◆

*[Joy] is an attitude, a disposition, a deep, settled confidence*
*that a loving heavenly Father is in control of the details of my life.*
JOSEPH ALDRICH
Discipleship Journal

◆

<u>          </u>
DATE


<u>          </u>
DATE


<u>          </u>
DATE


<u>          </u>
DATE


◆

*The joy of the LORD is your strength.*
NEHEMIAH 8:10

◆

# PERSEVERANCE

◆

We seem to believe that we won't fail if we know God. It's as if just being related to Him will keep us from the mistakes the rest of the world faces. We think that failure is reserved for blatant sinners or careless fortune-hunters. Christians, it seems to us, are guaranteed success.

Scripture says otherwise. Speaking about the responsibility of teaching and watching our tongue for error, James 3:2 boldly states that "we all stumble in many ways." J. B. Phillips paraphrases this verse to say, "We all make mistakes in all kinds of ways." It's important to realize that James is not writing to unbelievers. He's writing to Christians, to folks who will stumble in many ways!

Need some proof of our vulnerability? Who does the Bible show to us in their failures? Well, there's Adam and Eve who failed by eating the forbidden fruit. And how about Moses? He failed by losing control of his temper, striking an Egyptian, and bringing about his death. He also failed by disobeying God and striking a rock during his wilderness journey. David failed miserably in taking Bathsheba in adultery, murdering her husband, and then lying about his actions. Jonah failed by initially refusing to go to Ninevah. Peter failed by denying Jesus. Mark failed by abandoning Paul on his missionary journey.

Without a doubt, Scripture reveals that God's people can and do fail. We're going to make mistakes. Big ones. Little ones. Sometimes our failures will be due to deliberate, sinful choices of the will. Other times our mistakes will be innocent miscalculations. Whether mature or young in our faith, we can expect to stumble.

When we do, part of what matters is what we do after the error. Failure may surprise the weak and buckle them under its weight. But those who practice perseverance will see past an error to what can be learned from it. Perseverance is getting up and moving ahead again, in spite of past failure. And those who truly belong in God's family can expect a lot of opportunities to practice perseverance.

---◆---

### PRAYER

*Dear Lord, please convince my child that there is no such thing as a life free of failure. Teach him how You view failure: as a tool for teaching Your lessons about life. Help my child to learn to persevere in the face of failure. Help him to develop the attitude that failing is not necessarily a reason to quit, but always a reason to try again, even if in a different direction. Amen.*

---◆---

◆

*Consider it pure joy, my brothers, whenever you face trials of many kinds,*
*because you know that the testing of your faith develops perseverance.*
*Perseverance must finish its work so that you may be mature*
*and complete, not lacking anything.*
JAMES 1:2-4

◆

---
DATE


---
DATE


---
DATE


---
DATE

◆

*In all that God does with us, in all the puzzling and bewildering vicissitudes of life, His purpose is the development of Christlike character, of pure selflessness, of agape love. Failure may be a better instrument to achieve that than success. . . . If God is going to perfect Christlikeness in you and in me, it may sometimes involve the failure of our ambition, of our plans, of our dreams, of our hopes.*

PAUL BILLHEIMER
The Mystery of God's Providence

◆

---
DATE

---
DATE

---
DATE

---
DATE

◆

*Sin that's been confessed, wrestled with, and overcome is one of the finest teachers we have. Our struggles and defeats can increase our spiritual growth just as much as our victories—if we learn from them.*
DAVID SWARTZ
Dancing with Broken Bones

◆

_____
DATE


_____
DATE


_____
DATE


_____
DATE

◆

*No man is defeated until he gives up.*
ULYSSES S. GRANT

◆

_____
DATE

_____
DATE

_____
DATE

_____
DATE

◆

*Blessed is the man who perseveres under trial,*
*because when he has stood the test, he will receive the crown of life*
*that God has promised to those who love him.*
JAMES 1:12

◆

# WISDOM

What makes a wise guy wise?

In part, it's being smart. The Hebrew word for *wisdom,* "hokmah," implies knowledge. A person with superior mental ability in a given category is considered "wise."

But that's not all. "Hokmah" is most accurately translated "a skill for living." Commentators tell us that this word is used throughout the Old Testament to refer to the skill of craftsmen, sailors, singers, administrators, and counselors. In fact, in Exodus 28:3, God commands that the "skilled men to whom I have given wisdom in such matters . . . are to make garments for Aaron, for his consecration, so he may serve me as priest." Those who embroidered detailed and lavish robes for the priests of the Old Testament were considered by God to be wise. They had the knowledge and the expertise to put knowhow into action.

Translated over to the spiritual realm, wisdom is more than knowing truths about God. It is the skill for being able to apply God's truths to life in such a way that they make a difference in our thinking and in our actions. Such a view of wisdom affects the way we eat, think, and play. It changes how we listen and what we share. It alters our relationships in and outside of the family.

You won't be wise just by being smart. It's not enough to know just the answers to the struggles of life. Wisdom is knowing what to *do* with what you know. It's a skill for living life. And those who are interested in becoming wise guys will study life and then apply what they learn in the way they live.

---◆---

## PRAYER

*Dear Lord, please make my child wise. Give her both knowledge and the ability to know what to do with her knowledge. May she take the truths of Your nature and apply them in how she responds to Your will. May she ponder the realities of Your Word and integrate them into her actions. Make this child one who is truly skilled for living, not because she can quote a list of biblical values, but because she knows how to apply those values and truths to the way she lives. Amen.*

---◆---

◆

*The fear of the LORD is the beginning of knowledge,*
*but fools despise wisdom and discipline.*
PROVERBS 1:7

◆

_____
DATE


_____
DATE


_____
DATE


_____
DATE

◆

*Most of what I really need to know about how to live,*
*and what to do, and how to be, I learned in kindergarten.*
*Wisdom was not at the top of the graduate school mountain,*
*but there in the sandbox at nursery school.*
ROBERT FULGHUM
All I Ever Really Need to Know I Learned in Kindergarten

◆

_____
DATE

_____
DATE

_____
DATE

_____
DATE

◆

*He who walks with the wise grows wise.*
PROVERBS 13:20

◆

DATE

DATE

DATE

DATE

◆

*I'm always ready to learn,*
*though I don't always like being taught.*
WINSTON CHURCHILL

◆

---
DATE

---
DATE

---
DATE

---
DATE

◆

*Let the wise listen and add to their learning.*
PROVERBS 1:5

◆

# LEARNING TO LOVE

◆

*There are only three things that are eternal:*
*God, His Word . . .*
*and people.*
AUTHOR UNKNOWN

# LOVE

---
◆

Love may make the world go round, but not without a lot of work.

While serving as a missionary to Africa, Walter Trobisch befriended an African teenager and corresponded with him regarding a developing love relationship with a young girl. The letters were published in a book by Trobisch entitled, *I Loved a Girl.* In one passage, Trobisch shares a characteristic that is true of love in any language: Love is a skill that must be practiced in order to be perfected. He writes,

> There is no art without skill. Since love is an art, it needs skill. But every skill has to be learned and no skill can be learned without discipline.[1]

In another letter to his young friend, Dr. Trobisch teaches, "True love communicates. Love that finds no words to express itself soon dies."[2] In essence, he's saying that if we fail to put our love into action, we fail to love.

Trobisch's words ring with biblical truth. Recall John's words in 1 John 3:16-17:

> This is how we know what love is: Jesus Christ laid down his life for us. And we ought to lay down our lives for our brothers. If anyone has material possessions and sees his brother in need but has no pity on him, how can the love of God be in him?

By practicing love, we can perfect it.

There is a second way we can perfect love: by purifying our motives for loving. Bernard of Clairvaux, a monk from the thirteenth century, suggested four stages of Christian maturity. The first is "Love of the self for self's sake." This is the infantile self-centered stage we all know well. The second is "Love of God for self's sake." This is the place where we expect of God what we think is best for us. The third stage is "Love of God for God's sake." This is the goal of all praise and worship, that God will be glorified for His own pleasure. This is seen by many people as the ultimate in religious expression.

But Bernard offered a fourth stage. The last stage is "Love of self for God's sake." We are the Father's, and it is His pleasure that we love ourselves and become all that He desires for us. Once we reach this stage, Jesus' command that we love our neighbors as ourselves can become a reality.

Love is a skill that requires a lot of work. By practicing and purifying it, we can aim toward perfection.

---◆---

### PRAYER

*Dear Lord, please help my child learn to love others with the love You have shown him. Give him opportunities to perfect the skill of love. Offer him the challenge of practice. May he put his feelings of affection into words. May he express his commitment in action. And please, help him to perfect his love by purifying his motives. May he so internalize Your acceptance of who You've made him to be that he can readily accept and underline the potential in others. Amen.*

---◆---

◆

*Jesus loves me, this I know. For the Bible tells me so.*
ANNA B. WARNER
"Jesus Loves Me"

◆

_____
DATE

_____
DATE

_____
DATE

_____
DATE

◆

*If the core business of Life is to love each other as God loves us, then*
*a priority effort to play it safe interferes with the purpose of living.*
LARRY CRABB
Inside Out

◆

DATE
_____

DATE
_____

DATE
_____

DATE
_____

◆

*Love is patient, love is kind. It does not envy, it does not boast,*
*it is not proud. It is not rude, it is not self-seeking, it is not easily angered,*
*it keeps no record of wrongs. Love does not delight in evil but rejoices*
*with the truth. It always protects, always trusts, always hopes,*
*always perseveres. Love never fails.*
1 CORINTHIANS 13:4-8

◆

---

DATE

---

DATE

---

DATE

---

DATE

◆

*Love* enables *us to do what love obligates us to do.*
LEWIS SMEDES
Love Within Limits

◆

---
DATE


---
DATE


---
DATE


---
DATE


◆

*We love because he first loved us.*
1 JOHN 4:19

◆

# KINDNESS

♦

God wants His people to be good. He's pleased when our goodness illustrates Him to those around us. But goodness isn't enough. Reflecting on what she'd seen in too many lives, a little girl was overheard praying, "Lord, make all the bad people good and all the good people nice."

In addition to being good, we need to be kind. The quality of goodness has to do with the core of an individual, what he or she believes, what motivates him or her, who he or she worships. Kindness then takes that core and puts it into practice so that what is believed in private is expressed in public.

Goodness recognizes a need. Kindness meets it. Goodness stands against famines. Kindness sends money to buy food. Goodness knows the Bible teaches we are to care for the needy. Kindness goes to the hospital with an unwed mother and coaches her through labor and delivery. In Ephesians 2:6-7, Paul writes,

> And God raised us up with Christ and seated us with him in the heavenly realms in Christ Jesus, in order that in the coming ages he might show the incomparable riches of his grace, expressed in his kindness to us in Christ Jesus.

Then in Titus 3:4-5, he says,

> But when the kindness and love of God our Savior appeared, he saved us, not because of righteous things we had done, but because of his mercy.

Goodness realizes that there's a job that needs done. Kindness does the job.

George Mueller prayed constantly, "Lord, keep me from becoming a cranky old Christian." Because we've received God's grace, Christians can be good. But goodness must go beyond the mind. It must find its expression in kindness.

Kindness is not just for white-haired ladies with crinkled smiles. It's not just for the jolly drugstore manager who keeps a dish of candy on hand for hungry children. Kindness is the genuine demonstration of the goodness of God. Dear God, please make the bad people good and the good people nice.

---

### PRAYER

*Dear Lord, please teach my child to demonstrate goodness by being kind. Move her past the sideline of concern to the arena of action. As You work in her life to make her good—more like You—please make her nice as well. Amen.*

◆

*Be kind and compassionate to one another,*
*forgiving each other, just as in Christ God forgave you.*
EPHESIANS 4:32

◆

DATE

DATE

DATE

DATE

◆

*He who despises his neighbor sins,*
*but blessed is he who is kind to the needy.*
PROVERBS 14:21

◆

_____
DATE

_____
DATE

_____
DATE

_____
DATE

◆

*Kindness is not treating people on the basis of merit and justice
but on the basis of God's grace.*
GARY INRIG
Quality Friendship

◆

_____

DATE

_____

DATE

_____

DATE

_____

DATE

◆

*Make sure that nobody pays back wrong for wrong, but always
try to be kind to each other and to everyone else.*
1 THESSALONIANS 5:15

◆

_____
DATE

_____
DATE

_____
DATE

_____
DATE

◆

*I do not truly become kind until I seek not kindess but the source of
kindness. When I find the source, kindness becomes part of my character.*
LARRY RICHARDS AND NORM WAKEFIELD
Fruit of the Spirit

◆

# FORGIVENESS

◆

Forgive and forget. Is that what we're supposed to do? Is that what God does?

In Psalm 103:11-12 we read,

> For as high as the heavens are above the earth,
>     so great is his love for those who fear him;
> as far as the east is from the west,
>     so far has he removed our transgressions from us.

The Apostle Paul spells it out even more clearly in 1 Corinthians 13:5 where he writes that love keeps no record of wrongs. The word *record* here is an accounting term. An accountant keeps a record of debts by making a deliberate stroke of the pen in a specifically labeled column. When Paul writes that God's love keeps no record of wrongs, he means that an infraction is deliberately not recorded.

By God's example, forgiveness means forgetting. Saying "I forgive you" is one thing. Doing so is more difficult. R. Lofton Hudson describes just how hard it is for us to forgive and forget in his book *Grace Is Not a Blue-Eyed Blond:*

> People bury hatchets but carefully tuck away the map which tells where their hidden weapon lies. We put our resentments in cold storage and then pull the switch to let them thaw out again. Our grudges are taken out to the lake to drown them—even the lake of prayer—and we end up giving them a

swimming lesson. How often have we torn up the canceled note but hang on to the wastebasket that holds the pieces.[1]

As hard as it is, and as long as it sometimes takes to master, forgiveness means remembering to forget. It means forcing intruding memories of forgiven hurts out of our minds. It means tying back the hand that longs to pick a scab open, making it possible for the forming scar to heal the wound. It means refusing to dwell on wrongs that have already been reconciled.

Forgiveness means remembering to forget. That's what God does. That's what we must do for each other.

---◆---

### PRAYER

*Dear Lord, please help my child learn the truth about forgiveness. May he grasp what it really means to be forgiven by You. May he comprehend that You don't merely look the other way or wave sin aside as if it doesn't matter, but rather you cancel a personal debt. And, understanding this, may my child appropriate Your forgiveness so that he might forgive others. Teach him that forgiveness means canceling the debts of others and then remembering to forget the wrongs they have committed. Make him like you: one who forgets the wrong but remembers the forgiveness. Amen.*

---◆---

◆

*Bear with each other and forgive whatever grievances you may have*
*against one another. Forgive as the Lord forgave you.*
COLOSSIANS 3:13

◆

_____
DATE


_____
DATE


_____
DATE


_____
DATE

◆

*Real forgiveness means looking steadily at the sin, the sin that is left over without any excuse, after all allowances have been made, and seeing it in all its horror, dirt, meanness and malice, and nevertheless being wholly reconciled to the man who has done it.*
C. S. LEWIS
This Business of Heaven

◆

---
DATE

---
DATE

---
DATE

---
DATE

◆

*[Love] keeps no record of wrongs.*
1 CORINTHIANS 13:5

◆


DATE


DATE


DATE


DATE

◆

*God throws our sins into the depths of the sea. I like to think
that He puts a "No Fishing Allowed" sign there.*
CORRIE TEN BOOM
Not I, But Christ

◆

DATE _____

DATE _____

DATE _____

DATE _____

◆

*Expecting instant healing can be very disappointing.
Forgiving is like drawing compound interest.
You get gradual increments rather than one big bonanza.*
LEWIS SMEDES
HIS Magazine

◆

# TEACHABILITY

◆

What do you think?

Most of us aren't sure what we think about the complex issues of life. We ponder the pros and cons of a decision on either side of an issue, scratch our heads, screw up our faces, and look to our pastor for a definitive answer. We throw up our hands in frustration and run to the commentators to decide the situation for us. We exhaust ourselves considering the options and check out a popular book by a well-known evangelical and memorize his position.

It's easier to let someone else do the thinking for us. The professionals are better at putting thoughts into words that make sense. After all, they're the ones with the education, aren't they?

This attitude of dependency or mindlessness is common in our churches. The thinking that goes along with studying is hard work, and many Christians would rather let someone else do it for them. No matter how popular this attitude, I believe that when we turn our thoughts over to someone else's control, we cheat ourselves of growth in godliness—and of the sheer fun of making our own discoveries!

We need to learn to use our minds. Or, putting it another way, we need to determine to become students for life. Ignorance creates fear. It entraps and enslaves. When we don't know what we think, we're afraid to speak up. When we aren't sure what God says about a subject, we grow anxious and invent possible answers. When we think there is only one right answer to every question, we hesitate to explore the complexities of life.

Ignorance creates fear, but education liberates. We won't ever know it all. But we can know enough in order to live more effectively here. When someone questions our view of suffering, we can offer insight if we've given thought to this hard-to-understand subject.

It's wise to do some research and to glean from those who've done their homework on a given subject. Anyone who is serious about learning won't skip this step. But if we want to be students for life, if we want to grow in our understanding of God, then we'll learn to make up our own minds after we've considered the minds of others.

---◆---

**PRAYER**

*Dear Lord, teach my child to think. Make her Your student for life. Interest her in the hard-to-answer questions of her day. Plant in her a desire to find out for herself and to process what she discovers in the light of Your Word. May she never be satisfied with letting someone else think for her. Lead her to the education in You that liberates. Amen.*

---◆---

◆

*Do not conform any longer to the pattern of this world,*
*but be transformed by the renewing of your mind.*
ROMANS 12:2

◆

---
DATE

---
DATE

---
DATE

---
DATE

◆

*In our pressurized society, people who are out of shape mentally, usually
fall victim to ideas and systems that are destructive to the human spirit
and to human relationships. They are victimized because they
have not taught themselves how to think; nor have they set themselves
to the life-long pursuit of the growth of the mind.*
GORDON MACDONALD
Ordering Your Private World

◆

―――――――
DATE

―――――――
DATE

―――――――
DATE

―――――――
DATE

◆

*Real ongoing, lifelong education doesn't answer questions—*
*it provokes them. It causes us to see that the fun and excitement*
*of learning doesn't lie in having all the answers. It lies in the tension*
*and the stretching of our minds between all the contradictory answers.*
*It makes us think for ourselves. It frees us. It helps us grow up!*
LUCI SWINDOLL
You Bring the Confetti

◆

_____
DATE

_____
DATE

_____
DATE

_____
DATE

◆

*Arrogance and a teachable spirit are mutually exclusive.*
RICHARD FOSTER
Celebration of Discipline

◆

_____
DATE


_____
DATE


_____
DATE


_____
DATE


◆

*If you're planning for a year—sow rice . . .*
*If you're planning for a decade—plant trees . . .*
*If you're planning for a lifetime—educate a person.*
OLD CHINESE PROVERB

◆

# DISCOVERING GOD

◆

*Truth forever on the scaffold,*
*Wrong forever on the throne,*
*Yet that scaffold sways the future,*
*And behind the dim unknown,*
*Standeth God, within the shadows,*
*Keeping watch above His own.*

JAMES RUSSELL LOWELL

# GOD IS GOOD

When a loved one lies near death, and he is suddenly healed, we whisper, "God is so good." When an unexpected check arrives by mail in time to pay rent and buy groceries, we praise, "God is so good." When we gather together Sunday mornings for worship, we share testimonies, sing hymns, and think thoughts that applaud the goodness of God. What does it mean that God is good?

The psalmist writes of God, "You are good, and what you do is good" (Psalm 119:68). When the Bible says that God is good, it means two things.

First, God is good in His being. The word *good* means what is excellent in character or constitution. God's being is good. Ask a mom what she is teaching her child, and on the list will be something like "to be good." We have to try to be good. Psalm 14:3 reminds us, "All have turned aside, they have together become corrupt; there is no one who does good, not even one." Goodness is not natural to us. But God doesn't have to try to be good, because He is good. His being is perfect. God is good, first of all, in His being.

Second, God is good in His actions. When the Bible says that God is good, it implies that God is willing to act on behalf of His people. God does good things. His actions are always consistent with His purpose of conforming His children to His likeness.

Sometimes we enjoy His goodness. He's good to give us what we need to be happy. When our lives are full and we have what we want, we enjoy His goodness. At other times, we question His goodness. For just as He is good to give us what makes us happy, He is happy to give us what makes us good. When we're hurting over a relational wound, impatient over delayed answers to prayer, or confused over His seeming absence, we don't feel like God is good. But He is. His actions consistently push us to the point where we will eventually resemble Him. Sometimes that means withholding what we think we want in order to provide what He knows we need.

God is good in His being and in His actions. When we say "God is good," this is what we should mean: that He expresses His good character in good actions that are aimed at our growth and our conformity to Him. That's good. That's God.

———————————◆———————————

### PRAYER

*Dear Lord, please show Your goodness to my child. Help him to understand that Your goodness is not like his. You don't have to try to be good, because You eternally are. And help my child to grasp that Your goodness may not always look good. At times, he will experience the joy of pleasant circumstances, and in such moments I pray he will know You to be good. But when my child struggles along in situations that are tough to endure, show him that You are good then too. Amen.*

———————————◆———————————

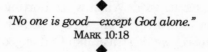

*"No one is good—except God alone."*
MARK 10:18

---
DATE

---
DATE

---
DATE

---
DATE

◆

*Often the circumstances we most desire to change are
the very ones that are doing the most good and that testify
most convincingly of our Father's goodness towards us.*
STEPHEN D. SHORES
Discipleship Journal

◆

---
DATE

---
DATE

---
DATE

---
DATE

◆

*And we know that in all things God works for the good of those who love
him, who have been called according to his purpose. For those God foreknew
he also predestined to be conformed to the likeness of his Son,
that he might be the firstborn among many brothers.*
ROMANS 8:28-29

◆

_____
DATE

_____
DATE

_____
DATE

_____
DATE

◆

*The greatness of God rouses fear within us, but His goodness
encourages us not to be afraid of Him.*
A. W. TOZER
The Knowledge of the Holy

◆

_____
DATE


_____
DATE


_____
DATE


_____
DATE


◆

*His goodness is Himself.*
LIZ THOMPSON
Moody Monthly

◆

# GOD IS HOLY

♦

These days, most folks don't fear God. The Creator of the universe is denuded of His power and replaced by a grand scheme of evolution. The all-powerful, ever-present Help is now seen as compassionate, but helpless to ease the suffering of our world. And holiness? Well. . . .

We waltz into worship on Sunday morning with little thought about the seriousness of the honor and praise we've come to bestow. We skip through prayer meetings, running down our lists and leaving. Where is the awe, the reverence, the holy respect God commands and deserves?

Gordon MacDonald, in an article published by *Moody Monthly*, quoted from A. W. Pink's *The Sovereignty of God*:

> The God of the twentieth century is a helpless, effeminate being who commands the respect of really no thoughtful man. The God of the popular mind is the creation of a maudlin sentimentality. The God of many a present-day pulpit is an object of pity rather than of awe-inspiring reverence.[1]

Then, in the same article, MacDonald asked the following:

> Is it possible that many of us who think our doctrine so perfect, our Bible knowledge so wide and deep, have forgotten the awesomeness of coming before a God who dwells in lofty places, whose name is holy, who inhabits eternity? Is it possible we have not given Him His rightful due?[2]

We ought to be afraid of God—not terrified, horrified, or petrified—but afraid. We ought to understand our relationship to Him and stand back in reverential awe of the fact that we even have one. He is God, the holy God, and there is no other like Him.

To be holy is to be the opposite of sinful. To be holy is to be pure and above all impurity. God alone possesses this quality. And any aspect of holiness we see in humans is put there only by God's redeeming and cleansing work. When Isaiah stood before God, he cowered in comparison and said, "Woe to me! . . . I am ruined! For I am a man of unclean lips, and I live among a people of unclean lips, and my eyes have seen the King, the LORD Almighty" (Isaiah 6:5).

There is no other like God. When we meet Him in private or in public, we ought to remember who He is and how we have the right to approach Him. Award-winning writer Annie Dillard comments on the inappropriateness of wearing straw and velvet hats in church in her book *Teaching a Stone to Talk*:

> We should all be wearing crash helmets. Ushers should issue life preservers and signal flares; they should lash us to our pews. For the sleeping god may wake some day and take offense, or the waking god may draw us out to where we can never return.[2]

Pick up your Bible, but whether you head to the back porch or to the pew on Sunday morning, proceed with care.

◆

### PRAYER

*Dear Lord, impress Your holiness upon my child. Teach her that while You gladly receive her as Your treasured loved one, Your presence is not to be entered lightly. Show her Your separateness, Your splendor and righteousness. Let her come to see Your singular purity even if that means she sees her complete sinfulness. Amen.*

◆

◆

*Much of our difficulty . . . comes from our unwillingness*
*to take God as He is and adjust our lives accordingly.*
*We insist on trying to make Him in our image.*
A. W. TOZER
The Pursuit of God

◆

_____
DATE


_____
DATE


_____
DATE


_____
DATE

◆

*Earth's crammed with heaven,*
*and every common bush aflame with God.*
*But only those who see take off their shoes.*
*The rest sit round it and pluck blackberries.*
ELIZABETH BARRETT BROWNING

◆

_____
DATE


_____
DATE


_____
DATE


_____
DATE

◆

*"Holy, holy, holy*
*is the Lord God Almighty,*
*who was, and is, and is to come."*
REVELATION 4:8

◆

———————
DATE


———————
DATE


———————
DATE


———————
DATE

◆

*Holiness is much more than a set of rules against sin.*
*Holiness must be seen as the opposite of sin.*
CHARLES COLSON
Loving God

◆

DATE

DATE

DATE

DATE

◆

*Only God is holy, just as only people are human.*
*God's holiness is his godness. To speak of anything else as holy*
*is to say that it has God's mark upon it.*
FREDERICK BUECHNER
Wishful Thinking

◆

# GOD IS GRACIOUS

◆

*Charis,* the Greek word for grace, is one of the most difficult Greek words to translate into English. Words like favor, beauty, thankfulness, gratitude, delight, kindness, benefit, are all derived from the root that gives us the word *grace.* If we have a tough time translating the concept into words, it's no wonder we struggle to comprehend what grace is in real life.

Digging through Scripture, we come up with a picture of grace. Grace is always tied to the heart and character of God. In Deuteronomy we're told that God drove out Israel's enemies not because Israel deserved His intervention, but because He chose to fulfill His word to His nation. In Isaiah we see that God longed to demonstrate His grace to a disobedient nation, and in Jeremiah God underlines His grace by promising again to bring Israel back from captivity.

Grace is God's character spelled out in undeserved love. In fact, grace is God, Himself, hanging on a cross in order to pay the debt we owe from sin.

Nicholas, the first Czar of Russia, would occasionally dress himself as a humble officer in his army in order to observe what was happening in his army. He had a favorite soldier, the son of an intimate friend, and he had placed this lad in charge of the monies used for soldiers' salaries.

The young man fell into bad habits and gambled away a huge sum, just a few rubles at a time, from the government funds. One night he received notice that an official would be by the next morning to examine the records and count the money he had on hand. The young soldier went to the safe, drew out the measly amount left, and sat down to make calculations as to the amount missing. After playing with figures for a while, he wrote under the numbers, "A great debt; who can pay?"

In utter despair, he concluded there was no way he could ever settle, and he made up his mind that in the morning he would take a loaded revolver to his head. In spite of the horror of the situation, he was suddenly overcome by drowsiness and slept.

While he slept, Czar Nicholas, dressed as a soldier, entered the room of his friend only to discover that he had been stealing systematically for months. His first thought was to arrest him. The next moment his heart went out in compassion. He glanced down, saw the pitiful question, "A great debt; who can pay?" and scrawled a word in reply. Then he left.

After about an hour, the soldier awakened and saw that it was long past midnight. He grabbed the revolver and lifted it, but before he pulled the trigger he spied a word on the sheet of paper that he knew was not written by him. The word was *Nicholas*. He compared the signature with official versions he possessed. "The Czar has been here tonight," he said. "He knows all my guilt, and yet he has undertaken to pay my debt. I need not die."

Grace is God. It is His undeserved love poured out in His unmatched Son, Jesus. It is God's character illustrated in our lives with the the scrawled signature of a cross.

———————————◆———————————

### PRAYER

*Dear Lord, please help my child to comprehend Your grace. May it not be just a dusty doctrine he mouths by rote during the recitation of a creed. May my child know Your grace by experience. May he come to see grace as You, offering acceptance in place of rejection, favor in place of judgment, forgiveness where condemnation is deserved. Amen.*

———————————◆———————————

◆

*For the law was given through Moses;*
*grace and truth came through Jesus Christ.*
JOHN 1:17

◆

DATE

DATE

DATE

DATE

◆

*For it is by grace you have been saved, through faith—*
*and this not from yourselves, it is the gift of God—*
*not by works, so that no one can boast.*
EPHESIANS 2:8-9

◆

_____
DATE


_____
DATE


_____
DATE


_____
DATE

◆

*Amazing Grace! How sweet the sound—*
*That saved a wretch like me!*
*I once was lost but now am found,*
*Was blind but now I see.*
JOHN NEWTON

◆

_____
DATE

_____
DATE

_____
DATE

_____
DATE

◆

*I do not set aside the grace of God, for if righteousness
could be gained through the law, Christ died for nothing!*
GALATIANS 2:21

◆

DATE

DATE

DATE

DATE

◆

*Nothing you ever do will ever make God love you any more or any less.
He loves you strictly by His grace given in Christ.*
HOWARD HENDRICKS
*quoted in* Discipleship Journal

◆

# GOD IS FAITHFUL

◆

A promise is only as good as the one who makes it. A dollar is just a scrap of paper, printed in green ink. What gives it value is the promise printed on it by the government. Because we take the government at its word, we believe the dollar's promise and the dollar becomes valuable to us. Similarly, the Bible is just a book. Its pages are loaded with words just like any other book. What gives it value are the promises represented by those words and the One who stands behind them.

When a man or woman makes a promise to us, we weigh the eventuality of the words by his or her character. The word of a doctor, a lawyer, or a minister has traditionally been trusted because of the high caliber of character seen in such professional persons. But now we've learned to question even the promises of such people.

When it comes to taking God at His word, we should likewise measure credibility by character. In his book *Prayer Power Unlimited*, J. Oswald Sanders writes,

> The validity and dependability of a promise rest on the character and resources of the one who makes it. . . . The holy character and faithfulness of God make His promises credible.[1]

One aspect of God's character that guarantees His promises is His truthfulness. Numbers 23:19 tells us, "God is not a man, that he should lie, nor a son of man, that he should change his mind. Does he speak and then not act? Does he promise and not fulfill?" And Psalm

12:6 says, "The words of the LORD are flawless, like silver refined in a furnace of clay, purified seven times."

People will break promises. Our experience with hurt testifies against the hope God presents in the promises of Scripture. An old saying suggests, "It's easier to believe a lie one has heard a thousand times than a fact one has never heard before." Rather than measuring the Word of God by the example of the fallen, measure it by the character of its Author. It is impossible for God to lie. He can be taken at His word because His perfect truthfulness stands behind it.

---◆---

### PRAYER

*Dear Lord, please give my child a glimpse of Your complete faithfulness. Help her understand that You are not like others she may meet in life. You are not even like her parents. Where others will disappoint her and even fail her, You and Your Word will be eternally faithful. Give my child the courage to risk belief in what will last: You and Your character. Amen.*

---◆---

◆

*God, who has called you into fellowship*
*with his Son Jesus Christ our Lord, is faithful.*
1 CORINTHIANS 1:9

◆

DATE _____

DATE _____

DATE _____

DATE _____

◆

*God has made an oath to us, and He will not break it. He will be faithful
to us; to do otherwise would be to violate His very nature.*
REBECCA MANLEY PIPPERT
Moody Monthly

◆

---
DATE

---
DATE

---
DATE

---
DATE

◆

*Yet he [Abraham] did not waver through unbelief regarding the promise*
*of God, but was strengthened in his faith and gave glory to God,*
*being fully persuaded that God had power to do what he had promised.*
ROMANS 4:20-21

◆

_____
DATE


_____
DATE


_____
DATE


_____
DATE

◆

*If we are faithless, he will remain faithful,*
*for he cannot disown himself.*
2 TIMOTHY 2:13

◆

---
DATE

---
DATE

---
DATE

---
DATE

◆

*Let us hold unswervingly to the hope we profess,*
*for he who promised is faithful.*
HEBREWS 10:23

◆

# Part Two

# STEPPINGSTONES: A CHRONICLE OF MEMORIES

*There is a deeper need . . . to enter that still room
within us all where the past lives on as a part of the present,
where the dead are alive again, where we are most alive
ourselves to the long journeys of our lives with all their
twistings and to where our journeys have brought us.
The name of the room is Remember—the room where
with patience, with charity, with quietness of heart, we
remember consciously to remember the lives we have lived.*

FREDERICK BUECHNER
A Room Called Remember

# QUESTIONS ABOUT GOD

◆

*The first key to wisdom is assiduous and frequent questioning. . . .*
*For by doubting we come to inquiry, and by inquiry we arrive at truth.*
PETER ABELARD

## QUESTION (include surrounding circumstances)

DATE

DATE

DATE

*Doubts must precede every deeper assurance.*
GEORGE MACDONALD
Unspoken Sermons

◆

*Don't start looking in the Bible for the answers it gives.*
*Start by listening for the questions it asks.*
FREDERICK BUECHNER
Wishful Thinking: A Theological ABC

◆

DATE

DATE

DATE

◆

*Look at the questions Jesus asked. He was a master at disequilibrium.*
*Look at His purpose: to get down to introspection which leads to choice*
*and action. Jesus didn't come to settle man's soul but to provoke it.*
HAROLD WESTING
Focal Point

◆

DATE

DATE

DATE

◆

*Never be afraid to doubt, if only you have the disposition to believe,*
*and doubt in order that you may end up believing the truth.*
SAMUEL TAYLOR COLERIDGE

◆

DATE

DATE

DATE

◆

*Doubts are the ants in the pants of faith. They keep it awake and moving.*
FREDERICK BUECHNER
Wishful Thinking: A Theological ABC

◆

DATE

DATE

DATE

◆

*The only foolish question is the one that is never asked.*
AUTHOR UNKNOWN

◆

_____
DATE

_____
DATE

_____
DATE

◆

*For without risk there is no faith,*
*and the greater the risk, the greater the faith.*
SOREN KIERKEGARD

◆

_____
DATE

_____
DATE

_____
DATE

◆

*Then he [Jesus] said to Thomas, "Put your finger here; see my hands.*
*Reach out your hand and put it into my side. Stop doubting and believe."*
JOHN 20:27

◆

# PRAYERS

---

◆

---

*All who have walked with God have viewed prayer*
*as the main business of their lives.*
RICHARD FOSTER
Celebration of Discipline

## PRAYER (include surrounding circumstances)

---

DATE

---

DATE

---

DATE

◆

*"I am the vine; you are the branches. If a man remains in me and I in him,
he will bear much fruit; apart from me you can do nothing."*
JOHN 15:5

◆

_____

DATE

_____

DATE

_____

DATE

◆

*The LORD is near to all who call on him,
to all who call on him in truth.*
PSALM 145:18

◆

_____

DATE

_____

DATE

_____

DATE

*Do not be anxious about anything, but in everything, by prayer and petition, with thanksgiving, present your requests to God.*
PHILIPPIANS 4:6

---
DATE



---
DATE



---
DATE



*You do not have, because you do not ask God.*
JAMES 4:2

---
DATE



---
DATE



---
DATE

◆

*Ask and you will receive, and your joy will be complete.*
JOHN 16:24

◆

DATE
_____

DATE
_____

DATE
_____

DATE
_____

DATE
_____

DATE
_____

# FAVORITE BIBLE STORIES
# AND VERSES

◆

*God did not write a book and send it by messenger to be read at a distance
by unaided minds. He spoke a Book and lives in His spoken words,
constantly speaking His words and causing them to persist across the years.*
A. W. TOZER
The Pursuit of God

## FAVORITE STORY OR VERSE (include explanation)

_____
DATE

_____
DATE

_____
DATE

◆

*Tell me the stories of Jesus, I love to hear;*
*Things I would like Him to tell me if He were here.*
WILLIAM H. PARKER

◆

DATE

DATE

DATE

◆

*For the word of God is living and active. Sharper than any double-edged*
*sword, it penetrates even to dividing soul and spirit, joints and marrow;*
*it judges the thoughts and attitudes of the heart.*
HEBREWS 4:12

◆

DATE

DATE

DATE

◆

*All Scripture is God-breathed and is useful for teaching, rebuking,
correcting and training in righteousness, so that the man of God
may be thoroughly equipped for every good work.*
2 TIMOTHY 3:16

◆

DATE _____

DATE _____

DATE _____

◆

*The riches of the Scripture do not lie on the surface
where they can be gathered like pebbles. The wealth of the Bible,
like diamonds, demands that we dig for it.*
HADDON ROBINSON
Focal Point

◆

DATE _____

DATE _____

DATE _____

# MEANINGFUL CHURCH EXPERIENCES

◆

*I'm so glad I'm a part of the family of God!*
BILL AND GLORIA GAITHER

## EXPERIENCE AND EXPLANATION

DATE

DATE

DATE

◆

*Now you are the body of Christ, and each one of you is a part of it.*
1 CORINTHIANS 12:27

◆

_____
DATE

_____
DATE

_____
DATE

◆

*Every day they continued to meet together in the temple courts.*
*They broke bread . . . together with glad and sincere hearts,*
*praising God and enjoying the favor of all the people.*
ACTS 2:46-47

◆

_____
DATE

_____
DATE

_____
DATE

◆

*And let us consider how we may spur one another on toward love
and good deeds. Let us not give up meeting together,
as some are in the habit of doing, but let us encourage one another—
and all the more as you see the Day approaching.*
HEBREWS 10:24-25

◆

———————
DATE

———————
DATE

———————
DATE

———————
DATE

———————
DATE

———————
DATE

# SIGNIFICANT MINISTRY EXPERIENCES

◆

*Do not merely listen to the word,
and so deceive yourselves. Do what it says.*
JAMES 1:22

## MINISTRY INVOLVEMENT
(include place, persons, and memorable lessons)

---
DATE

---
DATE

---
DATE

♦

*What good is it, my brothers,
if a man claims to have faith but has no deeds?*
JAMES 2:14

♦

DATE _____


DATE _____


DATE _____


♦

*Suppose a brother or sister is without clothes and daily food. If one of
you says to him, "Go, I wish you well; keep warm and well fed," but does
nothing about his physical needs, what good is it? In the same way,
faith by itself, if it is not accompanied by action, is dead.*
JAMES 2:15-17

♦

DATE _____


DATE _____


DATE _____

◆

*"For I was hungry and you gave me something to eat,*
*I was thirsty and you gave me something to drink,*
*I was a stranger and you invited me in,*
*I needed clothes and you clothed me,*
*I was sick and you looked after me,*
*I was in prison and you came to visit me."*
MATTHEW 25:35-36

◆

_____
DATE


_____
DATE


_____
DATE


_____
DATE


_____
DATE

# MENTORS

*[Mentors] rarely entered my world that they did not provide . . .*
*a growth point. And they rarely left my world at the conclusion*
*of an encounter that I did not feel lifted, impelled to greater growth,*
*and more aware of both flaws and possibilities.*
GORDON MACDONALD
Restoring Your Spiritual Passion

## MENTOR'S CONTRIBUTION TO LIFE

_____     _____
DATE                MENTOR

_____     _____
DATE                MENTOR

_____     _____
DATE                MENTOR

◆

*We have not stopped praying for you and asking God*
*to fill you with the knowledge of his will*
*through all spiritual wisdom and understanding.*
COLOSSIANS 1:9

◆

_____     _____
DATE            MENTOR



_____     _____
DATE            MENTOR



_____     _____
DATE            MENTOR



_____     _____
DATE            MENTOR



_____     _____
DATE            MENTOR




◆

*We proclaim him, admonishing and teaching everyone*
*with all wisdom,*
*so that we may present everyone perfect in Christ.*
COLOSSIANS 1:28

◆

# SIGNIFICANT LOSSES

*When you have nothing left but God,
you begin to learn that God is enough.*
AUTHOR UNKNOWN

## DESCRIPTION OF LOSS
### (include memorable observations and lessons)

_____
DATE


_____
DATE


_____
DATE

◆

*My grace is sufficient for you, for my power is made perfect in weakness.*
2 CORINTHIANS 12:9

◆

_____
DATE


_____
DATE


_____
DATE


◆

*We come into this world with our fingers curled and only slowly,*
*by repeated practice, do we learn to open our hands.*
*It takes a great deal of dying to get us ready to live.*
VIRGINIA STEM OWENS
Wind River Winter

◆

_____
DATE


_____
DATE


_____
DATE

*Jesus wept.*
JOHN 11:35

---

DATE

---

DATE

---

DATE

*The next time you are called to suffer, pay attention. It may be the closest you'll ever get to God. Watch closely. It could very well be that the hand that extends itself to lead you out of the fog is a pierced one.*
MAX LUCADO
No Wonder They Call Him the Savior

---

DATE

---

DATE

---

DATE

# THE MEANING OF CHRISTMAS

---

*Joy to the world! The Lord is come: Let earth receive her King;*
*let every heart prepare Him room; and heaven and nature sing. . . .*
ISAAC WATTS

## PROCESSING THE MEANING OF CHRISTMAS
(journal each year)

---
DATE

---
DATE

---
DATE

◆

*"For God so loved the world that he gave his one and only Son,
that whoever believes in him shall not perish but have eternal life."*
JOHN 3:16

◆

---
DATE


---
DATE


---
DATE

*The hinge of history is on the door of a Bethlehem stable.*
RALPH W. SOCKMAN

◆

---
DATE


---
DATE


---
DATE

♦

*For to us a child is born, to us a son is given, and the government*
*will be on his shoulders. And he will be called Wonderful Counselor,*
*Mighty God, Everlasting Father, Prince of Peace.*
ISAIAH 9:6

♦

_____
DATE

_____
DATE

_____
DATE

♦

*What can I give Him poor as I am? If I were a shepherd, I would give Him*
*a lamb, if I were a Wise Man, I would do my part—*
*But what can I give Him, Give my heart.*
CHRISTINA G. ROSSETTI

♦

_____
DATE

_____
DATE

_____
DATE

◆

*There were only a few shepherds at the first Bethlehem, and it is the same now. The ox and ass understood more of the first Christmas than the high priests in Jerusalem. And it is the same today.*
THOMAS MERTON
Eerdman's Book of Christian Classics

◆

———————
DATE

———————
DATE

———————
DATE

◆

*I will honor Christmas in my heart, and try to keep it all the year.*
CHARLES DICKENS

◆

———————
DATE

———————
DATE

———————
DATE

# THE MEANING OF EASTER

*Jesus Christ is risen today, Alleluia!*
CHARLES WESLEY

## PROCESSING THE MEANING OF EASTER
(journal each year)

_____
DATE

_____
DATE

_____
DATE

*"He is not here; he has risen, just as he said."*
MATTHEW 28:6

*"Remember how he told you, while he was still with you in Galilee:
'The Son of Man must be delivered into the hands of sinful men,
be crucified and on the third day be raised again.'"*
LUKE 24:6-7

◆

---
DATE


---
DATE


---
DATE


◆

*And if Christ has not been raised, our preaching is useless
and so is your faith.*
1 CORINTHIANS 15:14

◆

---
DATE


---
DATE


---
DATE

◆

*How could I ever have dreamed so sweet a morning after so dark a night?*
ELIZABETH ROONEY
A Widening Light: Poems of the Incarnation

◆

———————
DATE

———————
DATE

———————
DATE

◆

*"Destroy this temple, and I will raise it again in three days."*
JOHN 2:19

◆

———————
DATE

———————
DATE

———————
DATE

◆

*How foolish you are, and how slow of heart to believe*
*all that the prophets have spoken! Did not the Christ*
*have to suffer these things and then enter his glory?*
LUKE 24:25-26

◆

DATE

DATE

DATE

◆

*When he had led them out to the vicinity of Bethany, he lifted up*
*his hands and blessed them. While he was blessing them,*
*he left them and was taken up into heaven.*
LUKE 24:50-51

◆

DATE

DATE

DATE

# SALVATION

◆

*If you confess with your mouth, "Jesus is Lord," and believe in your heart that God raised him from the dead, you will be saved.*
ROMANS 10:9

## IMMEDIATE EVENTS
(What led up to a decision to trust Jesus as Lord and Savior?)

—————————
DATE

—————————
DATE

—————————
DATE

◆

*"I tell you the truth, anyone who will not receive the kingdom of God
like a little child will never enter it."*
MARK 10:15

◆

# CIRCUMSTANCES
(Describe the circumstances surrounding this decision.)

---------------
DATE

◆

*For it is by grace you have been saved, through faith—and this not from yourselves, it is the gift of God—not by works, so that no one can boast.*
EPHESIANS 2:8-9

◆

## RECORD THE DECISION ITSELF
(include the setting, people who were present, time of day, comments made by the child, etc.)

_____
DATE

# BAPTISM

*Or don't you know that all of us who were baptized into Christ Jesus
were baptized into his death? We were therefore buried with him
through baptism into death in order that, just as Christ was raised
from the dead through the glory of the Father, we too may live a new life.*
ROMANS 6:3-4

DATE                CHURCH

## A DESCRIPTION OF THE SPECIAL DAY

# FRIENDS AND RELATIVES PRESENT

# COMMENTS MADE BY THE PASTOR/MINISTER

# OTHERS INSIGHTS OR MEMORIES

# CHURCH MEMBERSHIP

◆

*Blest be the tie that binds our hearts in Christian love;*
*The fellowship of kindred minds is like to that above.*
JOHN FAWCETT

_____     _____

DATE                          CHURCH

## PREPARATION FOR MEMBERSHIP AND RESPONSE

## FRIENDS AND RELATIVES PRESENT

## COMMENTS MADE BY THE PASTOR/MINISTER

## OTHER INSIGHTS OR MEMORIES

## PREPARATION FOR MEMBERSHIP AND RESPONSE

### FRIENDS AND RELATIVES PRESENT

### COMMENTS MADE BY THE PASTOR/MINISTER

### OTHER INSIGHTS OR MEMORIES

# ROAD SIGNS FOR A SAFE JOURNEY

◆

Road signs help identify the path, warn us of what to expect, and point out guidelines we should follow for a safe journey. This appendix is included to offer such "road signs" for your child's spiritual journey. By familiarizing yourself with the various stages of mental, social, and moral development, you'll be better equipped to interpret your child's progress in his journey toward God.[1]

## MENTAL DEVELOPMENT
Jean Piaget theorized that all children progress through four basic periods along the path of mental development.

| STAGE | DESCRIPTION |
|---|---|
| Sensorimotor (birth to 2 years) | The child encounters his world in terms of action. There is a lack of object permanence: when someone is out of sight, in the child's mind he has disappeared and no longer exists. (No wonder a child hollers when Mom and Dad leave for a night out!) As the child learns to control his own body during the first two years of his life, he acquires the ability to mentally represent objects that are no longer present physically. |

| STAGE | DESCRIPTION |
|---|---|
| Preoperational (2-7 years) | The child encounters his world in terms of thoughts. With the emergence of language, the child continues to represent his world mentally. But his thinking is dominated by his own perspective. (When a six-year-old says she is right, there is no persuading otherwise.) |
| Concrete Operational (7-11 years) | The child encounters the world in terms of relations. Logical thinking is applied to solve concrete problems. (Science fairs with fifth-graders are a scene where proof *must* be demonstrated!) |
| Formal Operations (11 years and up) | The child encounters the world in terms of theories. At last, he is capable of abstract, complex, mature thought. (Ah . . . the joys of dissecting the great truths of life—and being understood.) |

## SOCIAL DEVELOPMENT

Erik Erikson suggested that our psychological development is the result of an interaction between our biological needs and the social forces we encounter in everyday life. Development proceeds through eight stages. In each stage, we are confronted with a basic crisis that can be resolved in one of two ways.

| STAGE | CRISIS |
|---|---|
| Stage 1 (birth to 1 year) | Trust versus Mistrust Can I trust the world? If Mom leaves, will she return? If I cry, will my needs be met? |
| Stage 2 (2-3 years) | Autonomy versus Shame and Doubt Can I control my own behavior? |

Can I learn to obey? Can I stop the fit, keep the bed dry, eat my peas?

| Stage 3<br>(4-5 years) | Initiative versus Guilt<br>Can I explore my limits and become independent of my parents?<br>Will Dad answer me if I ask "why" again? |

Stage 3
(4-5 years)

Initiative versus Guilt
Can I explore my limits and become independent of my parents?
   Will Dad answer me if I ask "why" again?

Stage 4
(6-11 years)

Industry versus Inferiority
Can I master the necessary skills to adapt?
   Will I be able to learn to read? Will math begin to make sense? Will it be okay to ask questions when it doesn't?

Stage 5
(12-18 years)

Identity versus Role Confusion
Who am I?
   What do I think about issues like suicide, drugs, abortion, pollution? What does it mean to know Christ?

Stage 6
(young adulthood)

Intimacy versus Isolation
Can I give myself fully to another?
   Will I be able to trust another with my deepest self? When the going gets tough, will I choose to stay?

Stage 7
(adulthood)

Generativity versus Stagnation
What can I offer succeeding generations?
   Will my life make a difference? Is my work worth the effort?

Stage 8
(maturity)

Integrity versus Despair
Have I found contentment and satisfaction through my life's work and play?
   Will God greet me with, "Well done, my good and faithful servant"?

## MORAL DEVELOPMENT

Lawrence Kohlberg has found evidence to suggest that morality (ideals or rules that govern human conduct) develops in stages. Individuals usually progress from one stage to the next, though few actually arrive at the most sophisticated level of morality.

| | |
|---|---|
| **LEVEL ONE**<br>Step 1 | **PREMORAL—birth to 7 years**<br>Good equals what is pleasant. Bad equals what is painful. Rules are obeyed in order to avoid painful punishment.<br>     "Okay! I'll share my toys! Just don't spank!" |
| Step 2 | Right and wrong are judged on the basis of what pleases (and usually pleases the self). Rules are obeyed to obtain rewards and have favors returned.<br>     "If I share my treats, will you share yours?" |
| **LEVEL TWO**<br>Step 1 | **CONVENTIONAL—7 to 15 years**<br>Good boy/girl morality. Consideration of others enters the picture with high importance placed on the approval of others. Rules are obeyed to obtain approval.<br>     "If I let you borrow my ribbon, will you like me?" |
| Step 2 | Emphasis on law and order. Right and wrong judged by obeying the laws and authority. Rules are obeyed in order to avoid censure by authorities.<br>     "The Bible talks about giving one-tenth of our income. I'd better give $10 out of this $100 I just received." |

| | |
|---|---|
| **LEVEL THREE**<br>Step 1 | **PRINCIPLED MORALITY—15 years and up**<br>Accepted law. Individual rights are important as they relate to the majority. Rules are obeyed to maintain community welfare.<br><br>"Our government ought to do something to make sure the homeless folks have homes. I pay my taxes!" |
| Step 2 | Morality of individual's own conscience. Universal principles like the Golden Rule adopted. Rules obeyed to avoid self-condemnation.<br><br>"I need a new coat. But so does that old guy out there on the street. Maybe I'll give him mine." |

# NOTES

**INTRODUCTION**

1. Gordon MacDonald, *Ordering Your Private World* (Nashville, TN: Oliver Nelson, 1984), page 132.

**JOY**

1. Binion, Higgins, and Payne, "I've Got the Joy."
2. Andrew L. Acquistapace, "Do You Have the Joy?" *The Standard*, December 1986, page 36.

**LOVE**

1. Walter Trobisch, *I Loved a Girl* (New York: Harper and Row, 1962), page 16.
2. Trobisch.

**FORGIVENESS**

1. R. Lofton Hudson, *Grace Is Not a Blue-Eyed Blond* (Irving, TX: Word Books, 1972), page 93.

**GOD IS HOLY**

1. Gordon MacDonald, "Do We Monkey Around with the Everlasting God?" *Moody Monthly*, October 1981, pages 123-124.
2. MacDonald, page 124.

3. Annie Dillard, *Teaching a Stone to Talk* (New York: Harper and Row, 1982), pages 40-41.

## GOD IS FAITHFUL
1. J. Oswald Sanders, *Prayer Power Unlimited* (Minneapolis: World Wide Publications, 1977), page 33.

## ROAD SIGNS FOR A SAFE JOURNEY
1. This material is based on *Psychology: It's Principles and Meanings* by Lyle E. Bourne, Jr., and Bruce R. Ekstrand (New York: Holt, Rinehart and Winston, 1976), pages 305-324.

## WHAT'S A MOTHER TO DO?

A MOPS® group offers care and nurture to all mothers of preschoolers (infant to school age) by working through the local church to meet these women where they are. Since 1973, when the first group of women began meeting, several unique characteristics have defined the "best" MOPS experience:

- MOPS is a chartered organization. This maintains the integrity of the MOPS concept and insures that all chartered churches are in harmony with the MOPS Statement of Faith.
- MOPS is an outreach ministry to all mothers of preschoolers.
- The MOPS format of regular group meetings includes
  — Food and fellowship
  — Instruction relating to womanhood, marriage, children, and the home, all from a biblical perspective
  — Small-group discussion
  — Creative activities
- MOPS provides quality care and the opportunity for preschoolers to experience God's love through the MOPPETTS ministry.

- - - - - - - - - - - - - - - - - - - - - - - - - - - - - - - - - - - - - - - - - -

❏ Send me information about a MOPS group in this area.
_____

❏ I'm interested in beginning a MOPS group. Send me more information.
❏ Send me your FREE newsletter.
❏ I'd like to support the work of MOPS. Enclosed is my donation of
_____.

Name _____
Address _____
City _____ State _____ Zip _____

Clip out and send to:  MOPS International Inc.
P.O. Box 12190
Denver, CO 80212